Strategic ROADMAP

An intentional, memorable approach to achieving success

Andrew L. Shafer

Published by SIBBS
4314 Lawn Ave
Western Springs, IL 60558

First edition. 2020.

Written by Andy Shafer
Edited by Edward E. Green and Monique Keeley

www.andyshafer.biz
www.strategicROADMAP.biz

ISBN 13: 978-1-7351872-0-4 (paperback)
ISBN 13: 978-1-7351872-1-1 (ebook)

This book is dedicated to those who had the most to do with putting me on the right path and have made the adventure of life so rewarding:

Carol and Gary, Mary Lynne

and

Lauren, Rachel, Sean, and Kevin

Acknowledgements

Every book is a journey and every journey needs the right people to guide the trip to make it successful and help it arrive at the right destination.

This was especially true for the Strategic ROADMAP.

The journey started long before the ROADMAP framework emerged from my passion to help organizations successfully build and grow their business.

The strategies and experiences that shaped the insights that led to the ROADMAP were developed by working closely with executives and colleagues at Dow, NatureWorks, Cargill, Elevance, and SIBBS.

Especially significant in those experiences were Julie Fasone-Holder, Jim Stoppert, K'Lynne Johnson, Mel Luetkens, LaRae Lafrenz, John Salladay, John Stevens, and Pam Henderson. Their help and willingness to include me on their journeys made mine so much richer.

Tess Fennelly, Gayle Novak, and Ron Klingensmith helped polish the talk that resulted from the positive client response to the ROADMAP and has now been given in many different venues: company meetings, industry conferences, networking meetings.

Rob Spurling eventually (and probably unknowingly) provided the inspiration for the book in a conversation that pointed out how many organizations, especially non-profits he had worked with, could benefit from a simple, straightforward approach like ROADMAP.

Honestly, the talk was an attempt to avoid the increasing requests for a book to document the approach that clients and audiences kept making. I didn't want to write a book, but Rob's suggestions convinced me that the talk wasn't enough.

The initial draft flowed easily from the script of the talk, but a talk and a book are quite different destinations. It took the unfortunate change in conditions created by a pandemic to create the opportunity to revise, build upon and finish the draft.

Rob, John Salladay, David Hatfield, and Michael Huston all reviewed early drafts, providing helpful feedback. Finally, Eddie "redline" Greene and Monique Keeley significantly improved the final manuscript with their many suggestions and edits.

Each of you has my utmost gratitude for all you have done to shape the opportunities I have been afforded, the insights you have shared, and this book that emerged from them.

Thank you all.

Andy
May 2020

Table of Contents

Foreword

Where are you going with your business?

Are you a business owner? Business leader? Responsible for your company or business's success? This book will challenge, provoke, and inspire you – with a memorable approach – to drive your business to success.

After successfully building companies and businesses for both Fortune 50 and start up organizations, I started consulting and was surprised by how often leaders didn't know what "success" looked like for their business. Even if they had a point of view, they often didn't agree with other members of leadership on what it was or where they wanted to go.

Your business is on a journey. It's up to you to decide if it's headed to an exciting destination or just on a Sunday afternoon joy ride.

What's success for your company? Have you and your team selected and agreed upon your destination and the route to get there? Does everyone in the organization know the plan? Are they on-board and helping you get there?

Like any road trip, the destination for your business should be intentional. And like a road trip it should be an outcome of a plan, the strategy, to take you there.

You and your leadership should thoughtfully explore your options and their implications and trade-offs. Once you agree on the destination, communicate it clearly with those going on the journey with you.

Drafting a Strategic ROADMAP© will help get you where you want to go.

Since *Strategy and Structure*[1], the first book on strategy in English written by Alfred Chandler, was published in 1962, there have been approximately 20,000 business strategy books published. That's an overwhelming volume of material, approaches, and tools.

Despite all that material on strategy, my clients still struggled to develop and clearly articulate where they wanted to go.

What they needed was an approach to strategy that was **simple, comprehensive, and clear**. One that allowed them to utilize proven tools and approaches in a way that resulted in a clear plan that was easily recalled and communicated to everyone making the journey.

This need led to the development of Strategic ROADMAP, a framework for your strategy to be:

- Intentional
- Definitive and Clear
- Memorable
- Integrated for Impact

---

[1] Alfred Dupont Chandler. *Strategy and Structure: Chapters in the History of the Industrial Enterprise.* 1962.

The Strategic ROADMAP enables your strategy to be lived by everyone in your organization every day, allowing for faster decisions closer to the customer, and focusing your strategic investments to have optimal impact for the overall business.

Each letter in the word ROADMAP represents a critical element of a successful and effective strategy. Simultaneously, the two words that make up ROADMAP – ROAD and MAP – represent two critical activities required for success – planning and execution.

When building a road, engineers will survey the landscape, assess options, discuss trade-offs, and adjust the design parameters to develop the path to the destination based on what they learn. Your strategy should plan your route to success in a similar manner.

Building a strategic ROAD is an iterative process, it should involve a generous amount of discussion, debate and consideration of alternatives involving key members of your leadership and team.

Once the ROAD has been established, the MAP becomes your guide and tool for focusing on execution to ensure you're making progress toward the destination.

Successful organizations continuously update and adjust their strategies based on what's really going on. Successful strategies don't get put together once a year and then put on the shelf. Real life interjects and requires adjustments along the way before the journey is complete. Your strategy needs to be understood and lived by everyone on the trip – and their input effectively incorporated to help make the journey more enjoyable and successful. A well developed and communicated Strategic ROADMAP will help you accomplish this.

This book is an overview of the Strategic ROADMAP framework and the benefits that developing one will provide you and your business. It provides you a memorable, digestible, and straightforward approach to develop your strategy using proven tools and approaches. It is does not explore the individual tools in detail. As noted, there are over 20,000 other business strategy books that do that for you, some of which this book will reference, and you may want to use as you develop your ROADMAP.

Use this book to provoke and inspire you and your team, as a framework for planning and communicating your journey with your organization, and as reference to help keep you on course on your way to success. Good luck and Godspeed.

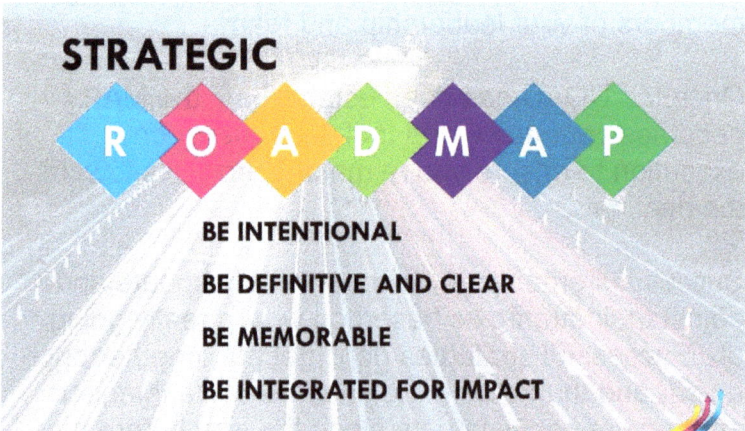

STRATEGIC

R O A D M A P

BE INTENTIONAL

BE DEFINITIVE AND CLEAR

BE MEMORABLE

BE INTEGRATED FOR IMPACT

Getting Started

Why strategy matters

Success isn't an accident. Oh sure, there's the occasional lightning strike and miracle, but most often success is the result of a clear, well thought out strategy and effective execution.

A robust strategy sets an objective – somewhere down the road – and allows everyone to know their role on the journey and when to do it. Consider auto racing. A driver and his pit crew work together with the goal of winning the race, from before the call "start your engines" to the checkered flag. While the driver and crew chief are responsible for the race strategy, clear roles and communication with the entire crew is critical to success. Conditions are constantly changing during the race, presenting both challenges and opportunities the team must respond to in order to be successful. A successful pit crew knows what adjustments are needed well before the driver arrives in the pit. They anticipate what's required for the next portion of the race and must execute with flawless precision to give the team an advantage and position it to win.

The same is true for your business. You and your team need a clear approach to creating advantages that give you an edge over competition and the ability to communicate effectively to adjust as conditions change.

Even if you're operating that way, it's highly likely that today's fast moving competitive and market dynamics are creating – or will **force** – change. Winning teams can adjust accordingly on the fly. They don't need to stop the race, return to the garage, and hold a meeting to discuss what to do next.

To operate this way, your strategy can't be a document that sits on the office shelf. It must be a memorable and consistent part of your business and team's regular activities; something that shapes and directs their daily activities – and that everyone in your business can use to make rapid, independent, yet consistent, decisions to stay ahead of today's fast moving and constantly changing marketplace.

Even when there is alignment on the destination, choices along the journey can lead to contentious leadership discussions.

Bottlenecks and (anticipated or unanticipated) detours can test the resolve of even the most aligned and committed leaders, especially when they haven't sufficiently discussed the logic and assumptions behind strategic choices that have been made. Too often leadership teams get focused on activities that will result in incremental improvements to the status quo, and discussions about the future lack depth, clarity, and specifics.

Unfortunately, when leadership is distracted or unclear, the organization behind them can lose their focus on creating value for customers, and correspondingly for the company. Instead, internal squabbling about asset and resource ownership or control takes the place of creating sustainable and distinct differentiation from those assets and resources.

An effective strategic planning process ensures leadership takes the time to discuss what's expected along the journey, options for getting to the desired destination, trade-offs among the choices and how resources will be committed along the way. Key objectives for any strategy should include alignment and clarity that allows empowered decision making throughout the organization and effectiveness that optimizes resource investment and deployment. The Strategic ROADMAP framework will systematically take you through this process, and give you an intentional, memorable, and clear output that will align and empower your organization.

What is strategy?

One of the challenges you may face is that strategy can defy definition. Since Chandler's initial introduction of strategic business management in *Strategy and Structure*[1] several different perspectives on it have emerged.

In one of the most comprehensive reviews of strategy formation literature and practices, *Strategy Safari*[2], Henry Mintzberg, Bruce

---

[1] Alfred Dupont Chandler. *Strategy and Structure: Chapters in the History of the Industrial Enterprise*. 1962.

[2] Mintzberg, Henry. *Strategy Safari*. 1998. First Free Press trade paperback edition 2005 ed., Free Press, 2011

Ahlstrand and Joseph Lampel chart the development of "schools of strategy." They point out that ten distinct points of view on strategy emerged from their extensive review of literature and practice.

Alternatively, Marcel Planellas and Anna Muni simply define strategy as "a decision" in their book *Strategic Decisions: The 30 Most Useful Models*[3] (which may be a useful resource on your journey to create your Strategic ROADMAP).

With the definition constantly evolving and so many different approaches to address the topic, it's no wonder that companies struggle to draft a useful and effective strategy. Accordingly, it's appropriate that we get started with the Strategic ROADMAP's definition of strategy.

---

[3] Planellas, Marcel, and Anna Muni. *Strategic Decisions: The 30 Most Useful Models*. Cambridge, United Kingdom; New York, Ny, Cambridge University Press, 2020.

The Schools of Strategy

The Design School	strategy formation as a process of <u>conception</u>
The Planning School	strategy formation as a <u>formal</u> process
The Positioning School	strategy formation as an <u>analytical</u> process
The Entrepreneurial School	strategy formation as a <u>visionary</u> process
The Cognitive School	strategy formation as a <u>mental</u> process
The Learning School	strategy formation as an <u>emergent</u> process
The Power School	strategy formation as a process of <u>negotiation</u>
The Cultural School	strategy formation as a <u>collective</u> process
The Environmental School	strategy formation as a <u>reactive</u> process
The Configuration School	strategy formation as a process of <u>transformation</u>

Mintzberg, Henry. *Strategy Safari*. 1998. First Free Press trade paperback edition 2005 ed., Free Press, 2011, page 5

ROADMAP's Strategy Definition

The Strategic ROADMAP uses the definition that

"Strategy is a plan that results from making choices which align activities and focuses resources to create sustainable and distinct differentiation and deliver value for targeted customers."

The nature of every journey, and ultimately the destination, are direct results of decisions made along the way. The same is true for your business. Making *choices* (or avoiding them) will directly impact your success.

The ROADMAP will help you achieve success by guiding your choices to be:

- Intentional
- Definitive and Clear
- Memorable
- Integrated for Impact

The two parts: ROAD and MAP

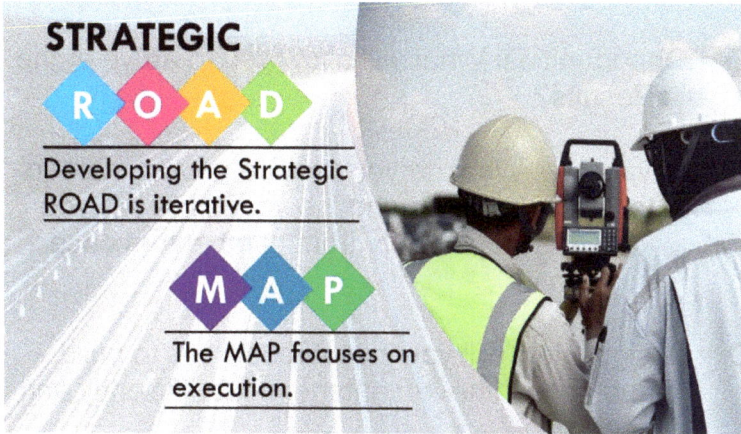

STRATEGIC

R O A D

Developing the Strategic ROAD is iterative.

M A P

The MAP focuses on execution.

The Strategic ROADMAP has two distinct parts. The ROAD is about planning and the MAP is about execution.

Identifying the strategic ROAD is iterative, so you can start with any of the elements. Work through them all until you're sure they work together and fit your business and circumstances to take you where you want to go.

Once the ROAD has been defined, the MAP allows you to proceed with confidence on the journey.

Part 1 of this book covers selecting the Strategic ROAD, challenging you to make choices about:

R = Results: Where are you going?

O = Opportunities: What will allow you to arrive at the Results?

A = Advantage: What do you provide your customers to compel them to choose you? How will you keep the Opportunity from competitors once you win it?

D = Design: How will you invest resources to build and deliver the Advantage most efficiently and effectively?

Part 2 of the book discusses the MAP, critical for successful execution of your strategy. In Part 2 we'll cover establishing clarity around:

M = Milestones: How will you know you're making progress?

A = Action Plans: Who is doing what, by when, and with something often missed – what resources?

P = Partners: Who can help you get there faster, cheaper, more enjoyably? What's your plan to engage them?

We'll get to the MAP shortly. For now, let's get on the ROAD.

Part 1: Selecting the ROAD

Chapter One: (R)esults

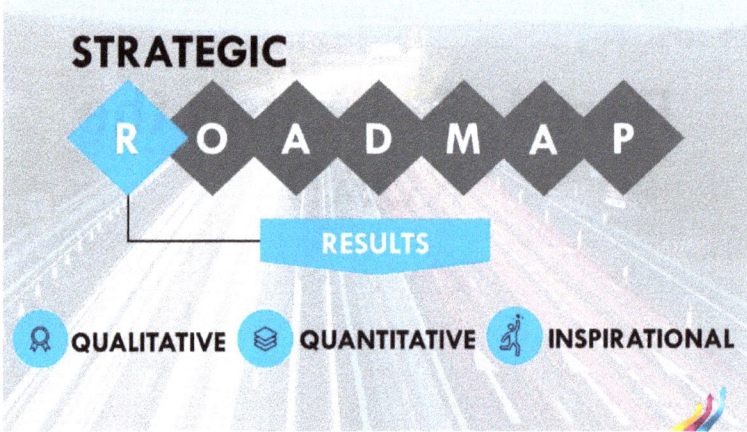

Define Success: Where do you want to go?

What is success for your organization? I'm constantly surprised by how often clients I work with cannot answer this question – including leaders!

Clarity on where you want to go on a journey is required to get there successfully and on time. It's equally critical for your business's success.

Your organization needs a clear description of what success looks like and the timing for it. This description should be qualitative and quantitative, defining what your business aspires to do and to become as well as the magnitude and time frame for success. And no one wants to go on a journey to an undesirable destination. It should also provide an inspiring vision, that energizes your team to strive for and accomplish more than you all thought possible.

As you make choices about where you are headed:

> Discuss the intent: is it to survive, to grow, to gain market share, to be more profitable or disruptive? Or are there other motivators beyond growth or profit? Social, environmental, and other non-economic drivers may be more important to you and your organization. Does everyone know what you want to accomplish?

> Are there parts of the organization that will need to change their priorities, roles or how they operate for you to succeed? Does your inspiring vision help them understand why? Are they energized, engaged, and excited about the envisioned future and the journey to seize it? Are you willing to support them to get to where you want to go? Be sure you're headed to the same destination.

> What will it feel and look like when you get there? How will you know when you've arrived?

> Successfully defining your "*R*" will mean everyone is clear and aligned on what it means.

Specifics are essential. The clearer you can be about the destination, the easier it will be for your team to help you get there. Be careful to define words like "leader", "best" or "first", which can be ambiguous.

- "Leader" in what?
- "Best" in whose opinion?
- "First" measured how?

If you use these terms, define them clearly and be sure that everyone knows what it will look like when they achieve them.

Remember, the "R" in strategy is both qualitative and quantitative. Your Strategic ROADMAP will need a corresponding financial plan. While generating "billions of dollars in profits" from "gazillions in revenues" by being the "best" is something too many companies want to do, that "R" is not a clear, qualitative description of the destination. Magnitudes or numbers alone won't provide the clarity that your team will need to guide their decisions on the journey.

Recall a memorable trip

Where did you go?

What was the purpose of the trip?

How did you travel – walk, car, plane, boat?

What was the route – direct or through intermediate stops?

Who went with you? What did they do on the trip/once you got there?

How did you know when you arrived? Describe the surroundings.

How long did the trip take?

Did you have to overcome challenges along the way (what did it take to do that)?

Why was it memorable? Something along the way, or once you arrived? Both?

What did you expect before you left? Did that happen? What did you learn?

How did you prepare before the trip?

What did you pack? Why?

Are there other things you wish you had done before leaving? What and why?

When you share your story of the memorable trip with friends, you can clearly articulate these types of details. But you need do it in a succinct and engaging manner, or your friends quickly check out and stop listening. When you've done it well, they often wish they had been with you!

The same should be true of your description of your desired business RESULTS. Describe the important elements of success in a succinct and compelling way to engage, excite and energize your team.

Define where you are now

Just like when you use a map, you can know your destination, but if you don't know where you're starting from the map won't be useful. Objectively assess the business's current status, performance, business model, strengths, and liabilities. If you're not sure where you stand, benchmark, get an outside perspective, or both.

It can be tempting to gloss over weaknesses or gaps or to exaggerate or magnify strengths, but remember, just like using a map, if you think you're starting from someplace that you're not it won't be long before you're not where you want to be or worse, truly lost.

What challenges do you need to overcome?

There are times when the organization should be focused on the horizon, good times when you'll have the luxury to shoot for the stars, and rough times when just getting to the next rest stop will be a huge success. Leaders who don't recognize the difference and adjust strategic objectives accordingly quickly lose credibility and the confidence of their organization.

Define the challenge that the organization needs to overcome to reach the destination. And consider the time frame that's required to overcome that challenge. For some businesses, it may be just surviving a big downturn or other disruption that's short term or temporary. At other times, those same businesses may have the luxury of being able to invest in traveling to new places. Incorporating the challenge to be overcome can help make your RESULTS clearer and more inspirational.

Why should we go with you?

And, as a leader, you won't be going alone. The destination and the challenge to reach it should be an inspirational and worthwhile place to go, so that others want to join you.

Of course, every business doesn't save lives or the planet, but how you as a leader think about the business you are building and why it's important can have a big impact on how others see it.

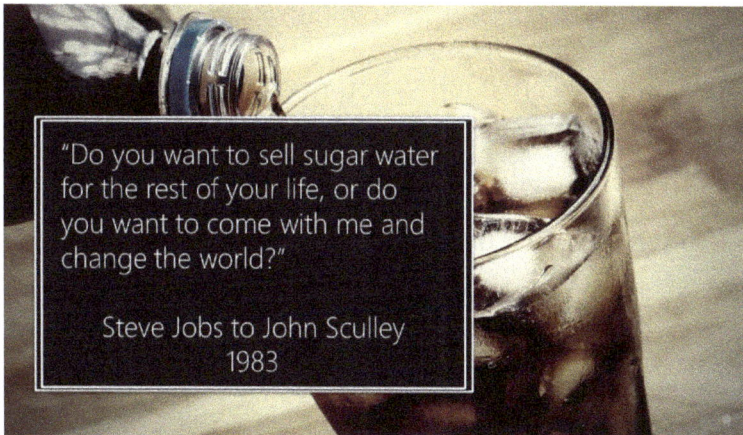

"Do you want to sell sugar water for the rest of your life, or do you want to come with me and change the world?"

Steve Jobs to John Sculley
1983

Steve Jobs did this masterfully when recruiting a reluctant John Sculley in the early days of Apple. Simon Simek talks about the "why" in a well-known

TED talk.[4] As a leader, if you haven't seen this talk you need to look it up. His golden circle model is a simple yet powerful model for inspirational leadership.

Let your RESULTS describe "why you are going, to where, and when you want to arrive." Clarity on these will give good people a reason to join you and enable them to help you get there. And as I am sure you know, having good people on your team is critical to success.

Questions to answer about your RESULTS

Have you discussed, debated, and defined:
- What success looks like?
- The timeframe to achieve success?
- Where you are?
- The challenges you need to overcome?
- Where you are NOT going?
- Your critical assumptions?

Have you described your RESULT:

Qualitatively? Does it clarify:
- Who you want to be?
- What you will do?
- How you will do it?
- Who you will do it for?

---

[4] Sinek, Simon. "How Great Leaders Inspire Action." ted.com, TED Talks, 2010, www.ted.com/talks/simon_sinek_how_great_leaders_inspire_act ion.

Quantitatively? Does it make clear:
- How you will measure success?
- When you want to achieve it?
- How you will know when you are there?

Inspirationally? Are you aligned on:
- Your values?
- Why you do what you do?
- Why it matters?
- Why customers want to buy from you?
- What makes you better?

Can you simply state: ***Why you are going, to where, and when you want to arrive***?

Tools to help define your RESULTS

Purpose statements
Mission statements
Vision statements
Values
Simon Simek's Golden Circle model
Abell's Three-Dimensional Business Definition
    model
Collins and Porras' Yin and Yang Vision model

Chapter Two: (O)pportunities

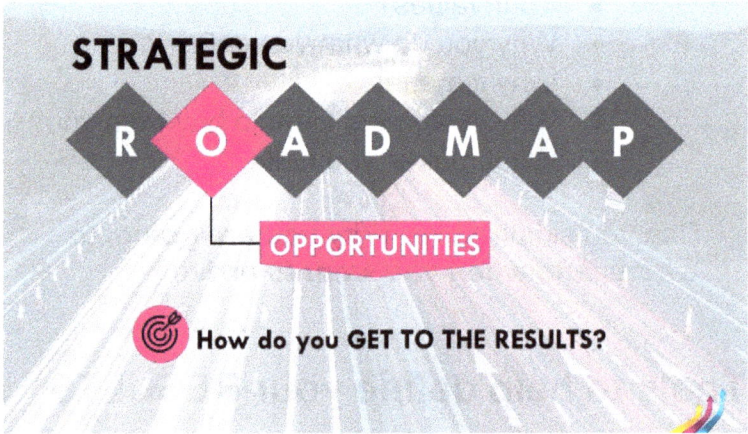

There are many paths

Once you're clear about where you are going, when you want to be there and why it's the right thing to do, how do you actually get there?

Every business has a variety of OPPORTUNITIES, ranging from doing something entirely new and different to not changing a thing.

What's the best path to your desired RESULTS? Remember, strategy is about choices. Like the destination on a map, there usually are a lot of roads to it – and many roads that will take you somewhere else.

Often, you can get to the same destination taking very different routes, using vastly different resources, and providing quite different experiences for those on the journey. A bike can be a great mode of transportation, but if you are in Chicago and success is in New York, it's going to take a while to get there. If you need to get there quickly, make a different choice.

The importance of landscape – and change

Any assessment of OPPORTUNITIES needs to start with an assessment of how the landscape is expected to change along the way.

Conditions have a huge impact on success. They may say "timing is everything", but it's probably more accurate to say, "timing and conditions are everything". In her book *You can kill an IDEA, but you can't kill an OPPORTUNITY! How to Discover New Sources of Growth for Your Organization* Pam Henderson defines opportunity this way:

> "Opportunity for revenue combines a receptive audience, the capabilities to create the right value, and the conditions that bring them together. The combination of the three is what ultimately yields revenue."[5]

---

[5] Henderson, Pam. *You can kill an IDEA but you can't kill an OPPORTUNITY! How to Discover New Sources of Growth for Your Organization* (Kindle Locations 415-416). Wiley. Kindle Edition.

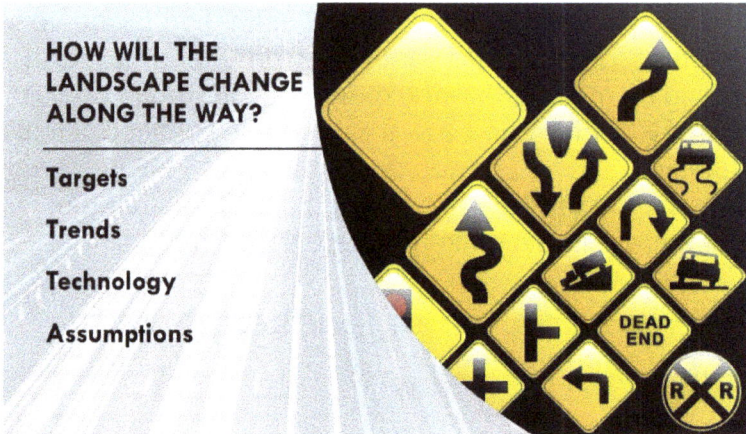

HOW WILL THE LANDSCAPE CHANGE ALONG THE WAY?

Targets

Trends

Technology

Assumptions

You're developing your strategy to ensure your *future* success, not to address today's conditions. Identifying OPPORTUNITIES requires an understanding of the changes taking place with your targets, the related technologies (solutions or capabilities to create value) and the conditions around them – the trends that are taking or expected to take place. The changes taking place with the target, technology or trends surrounding your desired destination create significant OPPORTUNITIES. Not paying attention to those changes can lead to significant problems.

Consider Eastman Kodak. The company was one of the first with digital photography technology and by mis-reading conditions (trying to launch digital photography too early, then dismissing it) the company has gone bankrupt while digital photography has now all but eliminated most other forms of personal photography.

In a chapter entitled "Why Leaders become Losers," Richard Foster, former Senior Partner and Director at McKinsey, wrote that most managers "assume that tomorrow will be more or less like today"[6] and that managers of companies who were among the best in financial performance "assumed that the day after tomorrow will not be like today". Even if you're successful today, being aware of how the landscape is changing is critical to your (continued) success. Change is the fountainhead of opportunity – for you and your competition.

Once you understand how change is affecting the targets, technologies and trends that make up the landscape to your destination, you can start to assess which OPPORTUNITIES can get you to your RESULTS.

What's needed to navigate the landscape?

Surveying the landscape will also allow you to assess your strengths and weaknesses relative to competitors, to understand your ability to navigate the changes with your current capabilities and which options will allow you to successfully deliver value.

Will the journey require a bike, a boat, a star-cruiser or maybe all three? Without a perspective on how the landscape will change you won't be able to assess the best options and OPPORTUNITIES for your organization. If you have the star-cruiser and the best

---

[6] Foster, Richard N. *Innovation: The Attacker's Advantage*. New York, Summit Books, 1986, p. 29.

option to your destination requires a bike you will need to make some adjustments.

Change is everywhere in today's volatile, uncertain, complex, and ambiguous world. In a second-quarter 2019 survey for its Emerging Risks Monitor Report, Gartner found that "pace of change" showed up as the top emerging risk, up from 2nd in the prior quarter of 2019 and 3rd in the last quarter of 2018, among 133 senior executives across industries and geographies.

> Seventy-one percent of respondents indicated that pace of change was a key risk facing their organizations. This risk was a consistent concern across industries, with particularly high ratings in healthcare, insurance, and industrials, with executives in these industries indicating pace of change as a top emerging risk with a frequency of 70% or higher.
>
> The concern around pace of change is driven by fears of being disrupted by nimbler competitors and a lack of clear avenues for growth. This risk can materialize through a rise in the number of new, disruptive competitors, a failure of the brand proposition to meet client needs or demands and executives not responding to macro trends and changing consumer needs.[7]

---

[7] "Gartner Survey Shows Pace of Change as Top Emerging Risk Concerning Organizations in 2Q19." Gartner.com, Gartner, 24 July 2019, www.gartner.com/en/newsroom/press-releases/2019-07-24-gartner-survey-shows-pace-of-change-as-top-emerging-r. Accessed 6 Apr. 2020.

If those executives were surveyed today about pace of change, do you think they would say things have slowed down? While it's hard to see what's around the curve ahead, there are plenty of approaches to assessing what you might face on your journey.

A critical first step when exploring the future landscape is to become aware of what is already taking place around you. Change is happening so fast that it is quite common for something you might believe to be in "the future" to be happening today at one of your customers or competitors. As discussed in Chapter 1, be sure you know where you are.

Extend your awareness to what might be possible. Consider all the key aspects of your business and how they might change. Explore alternatives – often future possibilities are in direct conflict; one possibility developing would make another impossible.

Discuss, debate, and decide with your team about what you believe is most important for you. Align on the choices you can make to be prepared and incorporate the appropriate actions into your ROADMAP.

An additional critical element of surveying the landscape is to take the time to establish signposts, indicators that will let you confirm the changes you expect take place when you expect them. In addition, capture your key assumptions.

Unexpected events can substantially reset what the future holds. In just the past two decades we've had 3 major events that have substantially reshaped the landscape: the terror attacks of September 11, 2001, the recession of 2008, and the coronavirus pandemic of 2020. Each of these events created real and significant changes that forced individuals and businesses to rapidly adapt to new and unexpected conditions. If unexpected events occur, the signposts don't appear when you expected them, or the assumptions that are built into your strategy are no longer true, your strategy needs to be reviewed and updated.

Finding OPPORTUNITY around the S-Curves

Foster addressed the problem of understanding how to assess where change can have a material impact on businesses:

> "In the world of business, limits determine which technologies, which machines and which processes are about to become obsolete. They are the reason why products eventually stop making money for companies".

In this context, he considered technology "broadly as the general way a company does business or attempts a task" and his point was that technology – and specifically the way you are doing things now – "always has a limit."[8]

He introduced S-curves, by plotting the "infancy, explosion and then gradual maturation" of the technology against performance on the vertical axis

---

[8] Foster, Richard N. *Innovation: The Attacker's Advantage*. New York, Summit Books, 1986

and the effort (funds) invested in advancing it on the horizontal axis.

Foster's S-curves are a useful way to analyze an industry for OPPORTUNITIES, particularly when overlaid with an adaptation of the "Ten Types of Innovation"[9] detailed by Larry Keeley. Keeley's Ten Types of Innovation can be distilled into your:

1) **Internal Business Configuration**: decisions regarding your internal business structure and operations

2) **Offering**: choices about the products and services your company provides

3) **Customer Interface**: how you elect to engage with your customers

Exhibit 1 plots Foster's "technology" S-curve as the solution that is being provided to the customer and market. The vertical axis redefines Foster's "performance" to be the "experience, benefits or value" the customer receives when using the given solution. Overlaying the concepts from Keeley on the horizontal axis, this Modified S-curve model allows consideration of both the investment in the solution and all the elements a company needs to bring it to market. This redefined model becomes an effective tool for looking for OPPORTUNITIES.

---

[9] Keeley, Larry, et Al. *Ten Types of Innovation: The Discipline of Building Breakthroughs*. Hoboken, Nj, John Wiley & Sons Inc, 2013.

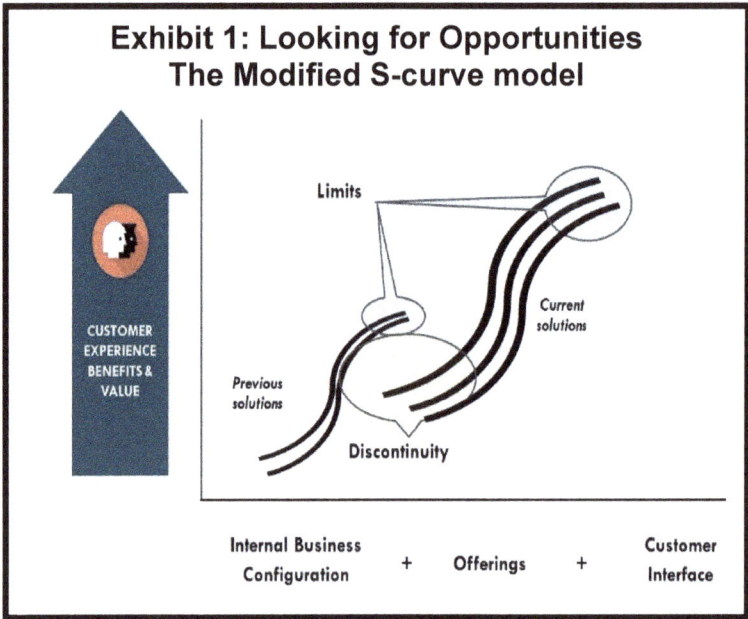

**Exhibit 1: Looking for Opportunities
The Modified S-curve model**

CUSTOMER EXPERIENCE BENEFITS & VALUE

Limits

Current solutions

Previous solutions

Discontinuity

Internal Business Configuration + Offerings + Customer Interface

Limits and Discontinuities

There are several ways to look for OPPORTUNITIES by leveraging the Modified S-curve model.

Foster points out that in mature technologies, at some point, the next increment of improvement comes at increasing cost – flattening the curve – thus ultimately defining the limit to the benefits customers will gain from that solution. This creates an OPPORTUNITY for new solution(s) that may provide improved benefit to customers. The shift to a new set of solutions is what Foster called a *discontinuity*. It is worth noting that often, an emerging solution initially provides lower value or benefit to customers initially as it has not yet been optimized.

When looking for OPPORTUNITIES, first consider where you are on the curve with the solution(s) you offer customers. Are the returns from your investments to improve your solution diminishing? Maybe you're approaching the limits of this solution and should invest in something where you'll get a better return.

If you're providing a mature solution that's well optimized and approaching the limits of the benefits it can provide, you might consider reducing investment in this solution to invest in a different choice, a new or emerging S-curve.

Conversely, if you have a newer solution that can be further optimized to provide improved benefits, or if there are large markets that haven't been fully penetrated you could choose to focus efforts in those areas with your current solution.

Another approach would be to consider what OPPORTUNITIES may emerge from varying the elements of the horizontal axis: Internal Business Configuration, Offerings and Customer Interface. How are solutions provided today? What elements make the Offering differentiated? What's not being done? What could be done differently or better to create value? What changes are taking place to allow or require any element or combination of them to be done differently, cheaper, better? Keeley's book *Ten Types of Innovation: The discipline of Building Breakthroughs*[10] provides an excellent discussion of how this can be done.

---

[10] Keeley, Larry, et Al. *Ten Types of Innovation: The Discipline of Building Breakthroughs*. Hoboken, Nj, John Wiley & Sons Inc, 2013.

You could also consider looking for OPPORTUNITIES by examining the vertical axis – customer experience, benefit, or value. How could it be different? Are there benefits or experiences of value that are unmet for some consumers? Ones that could be removed, but still be of value to segments of customers (i.e. a different customer benefit altogether)? Are conditions changing such that what constitutes benefit, experience or value will be different in the future? What could be done to address those needs?

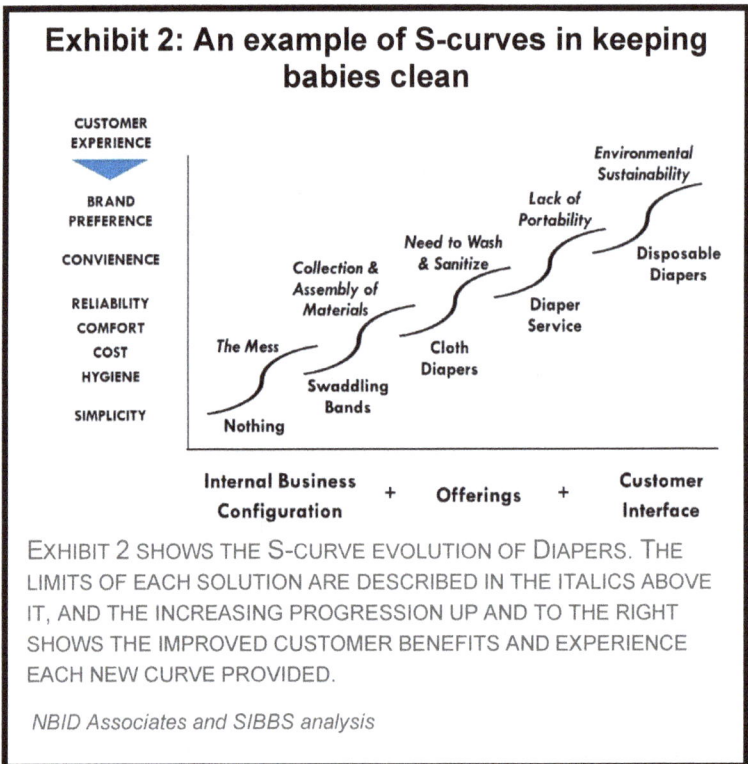

Exhibit 2: An example of S-curves in keeping babies clean

CUSTOMER EXPERIENCE

BRAND PREFERENCE

CONVIENENCE

RELIABILITY

COMFORT

COST

HYGIENE

SIMPLICITY

Nothing

Swaddling Bands

The Mess

Collection & Assembly of Materials

Cloth Diapers

Need to Wash & Sanitize

Diaper Service

Lack of Portability

Disposable Diapers

Environmental Sustainability

Internal Business Configuration + Offerings + Customer Interface

EXHIBIT 2 SHOWS THE S-CURVE EVOLUTION OF DIAPERS. THE LIMITS OF EACH SOLUTION ARE DESCRIBED IN THE ITALICS ABOVE IT, AND THE INCREASING PROGRESSION UP AND TO THE RIGHT SHOWS THE IMPROVED CUSTOMER BENEFITS AND EXPERIENCE EACH NEW CURVE PROVIDED.

NBID Associates and SIBBS analysis

Finally, someone on your team should be tasked with scanning for new, emerging solutions that might be developing. Has someone recognized a discontinuity and begun introducing a new solution that might not yet be good enough to compete with your current solution but may have the potential to do that – and maybe more? This would represent a potential OPPORTUNITY or threat to consider.

Focus is critical

You'll no doubt be able to identify several possible OPPORTUNITIES that can get you to your desired RESULTS, just like many roads can take you to a destination on a map. And while many of them may be interesting and worthwhile journeys, choices matter.

Most organizations have a limited ability to successfully focus, just like most garages hold a limited number of vehicles. How many vehicles fit in your garage? I realize there's always an exception; Jay Leno is reported to own 169 (and 117 motorcycles)[11] but for most of us having more than 2 or 3 vehicles is likely more of a problem than an advantage. It's great to have the flexibility of several different options in our garage, but consider that each one needs registration, insurance, service, maintenance, and repairs in addition to the cost of operation. There are considerable clearly visible and hidden costs.

Similarly, most organizations can only handle a few major OPPORTUNITIES. While optionality can be an

---

[11]   Berman, Nat. "10 Most Expensive Cars in Jay Leno's Car Collection That He Owns." *Money Inc*, 17 Aug. 2016, moneyinc.com/most-expensive-cars-that-jay-leno-owns/. Accessed 31 Mar. 2020.

advantage, those options will have hidden costs in addition to the visible ones.

Exhibit 3 shows a graph of an analysis done by researchers at MIT Sloan who looked at 494 companies traded on the 2014 Standard & Poor's 500 Index. They found that 78% listed three to five strategic objectives (with 143 companies either not listing theirs publicly – I hope – or not having them entirely – yikes!).[12] It's interesting to know that 69 companies had more than five strategic priorities. It's hard to imagine that employees can truly determine what's important if they have five or more priorities. A clear strategy will allow employees to have the benefit of you making true choices about what is a priority.

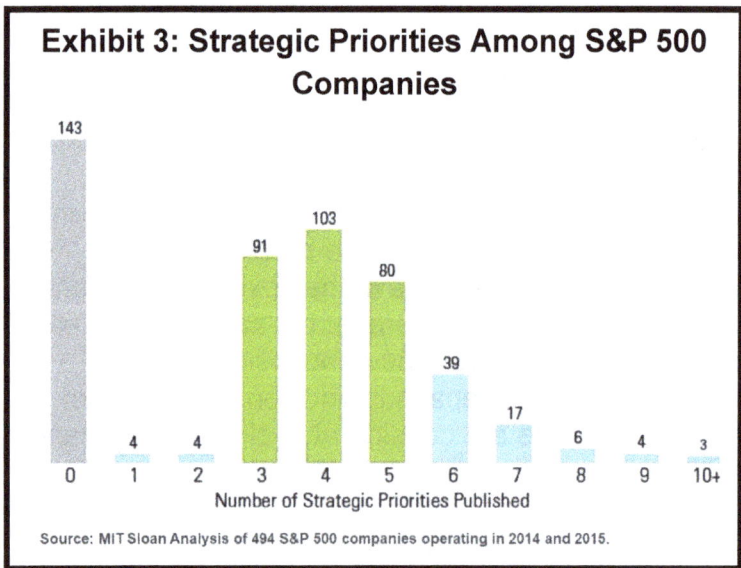

Exhibit 3: Strategic Priorities Among S&P 500 Companies

Number of Strategic Priorities Published

0	1	2	3	4	5	6	7	8	9	10+
143	4	4	91	103	80	39	17	6	4	3

Source: MIT Sloan Analysis of 494 S&P 500 companies operating in 2014 and 2015.

[12] Sull, Donald. "Turning Strategy Into Results." *MIT Sloan Management Review*, 28 Sept. 2017, sloanreview.mit.edu/article/turning-strategy-into-results/.

The power of 1

Attention is like light from a flashlight – the choice to illuminate something darkens something else. Your choice of an OPPORTUNITY will shine light on it, leaving other choices in the dark. Often just one OPPORTUNITY is sufficient for success. Some of today's biggest and most successful companies started with a single seemingly small OPPORTUNITY (the market for every new S-curves is small, as it didn't exist before) and those companies combined it with a compelling ADVANTAGE to achieve tremendous growth and success. Amazon, Google, and Walmart all started by focusing on a single OPPORTUNITY.

Walmart focused on putting department stores into rural communities, Google started with just search and do you remember when Amazon only sold books? Focusing on one OPPORTUNITY led each of them to becoming one of today's largest and most successful companies.

Explore and assess OPPORTUNITIES rigorously

Consider the market, purchasing considerations, margin implications and other aspects of the options you consider.

> Will they get you to the desired RESULTS? Are they the right size? Will they develop in the right time frame?

Do they fit with either who you are or
who you want to be? (Better if it's both!)
Can you establish an ADVANTAGE?
(more on that later – remember, the
ROAD is iterative)

Will/can they fit with where you decided
not to go when establishing the
RESULTS? Are you clear about the
priorities and focus?

Strategy is about choices. You want to get to the
desired destination (your RESULTS). Defining where
you **won't go** often helps make your choices clearer
for your organization and easier for them to stay
focused, getting you to your desired destination
sooner and more efficiently.

You may be tempted to dismiss the choice of where
NOT to go. But distractions and detours consume
both the resources and emotional energy you need
focused on getting you to your RESULT. One best
practice that can help provide clarity could be called
the "nearest neighborhood" exercise. Draft a sentence
that describes what is NOT in scope but that people in
the organization could reasonably believe to be
appropriate. Identifying the "nearest neighborhood"
will help make your choices about where you want to
establish boundaries more tangible.

Also, don't overlook that all choices have
consequences. What are the implications of the
choices you're considering? The trade-offs? Take the
time to consider the possibilities for unintentional or
unanticipated consequences and compare these
while you explore your options. Often there are ways

to reduce risks if you take the time to explore the possibilities. Just as importantly, you'll reduce the likelihood of contentious management discussions down the road by having had the discussions in advance.

Questions to answer about your OPPORTUNITIES

Have you discussed, debated, and defined:
- Your view of the landscape (the future landscape)?
- What changes are likely to impact your targets and technologies?
- The impact of significant trends?
- Signposts for key trends?
- Where your products/solutions are along the S-curve?
- The limits of your (potential) Offerings?
- The OPPORTUNITIES you want to focus on?
- How many priorities you're asking your organization to focus on?
- What's needed for success?
- The potential of new, emerging solutions?
- The consequences of your choices?
- Your critical assumptions?

Will the answers to the above questions:
- Get you to your desired RESULTS?
- In the proper timeframe?
- With the capabilities and resources you have or can acquire along the journey?

Tools to help define your OPPORTUNITIES

Future Proofing
Scenario Analysis
PESTLE Analysis
S-curve analysis
BCG Portfolio Analysis
Ansoff's Matrix
GE McKinsey Matrix
Business Model Canvas
Value Proposition Canvas
Opportunity Thinking
SWOT Analysis
Porter's Five Forces

Chapter Three: (A)dvantage

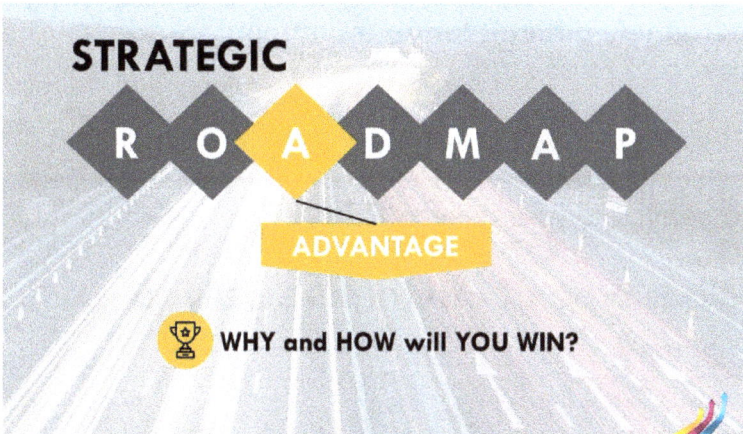

Making ADVANTAGE Intentional

Let's look at *"A"* your ADVANTAGE.

To win, you need to achieve ADVANTAGE in two ways:

> ➤ you'll need to **provide your customers an ADVANTAGE** for them to choose you and your OPPORTUNITY. What value will your customers receive, why can you provide it, how will it be unique?

And once you win the OPPORTUNITY with your target customers, you'll want to keep it so

> ➤ you'll need to **build and maintain an ADVANTAGE over competitors** who will want to take or improve on the OPPORTUNITY once you win it.

Keep in mind: **The best ADVANTAGE is one that is extremely difficult for your competitors to respond to or copy.**

First, let's look at getting your target customers to select you and the OPPORTUNITY you've identified to get you to your desired RESULT.

What type of customers do you serve?

After years of working with existing and new products and global experience in sales, marketing, and business development, I have consistently found 3 types of customers:

- Technology Enthusiasts

- Insurance Policy Buyers

- Parents of Screaming Babies

Technology Enthusiasts provide that hit of adrenaline that all of us crave. They love your product. They will enthusiastically embrace your Offering like a teenager with a new electronic game; consumed with exploring it and even providing in-depth feedback on how to make it better. But at the end of the day, there are a limited number of customers who will engage and embrace your offer in the same way. Your solution is interesting because it is the newest, latest, and maybe greatest (for the moment). But unless you'll always be the hip, new thing, Enthusiasts are not the core of the market. After the initial interest, adoption rates will be slow and likely not sustainable once the next new thing comes along.

Insurance Policy Buyers have concerns about their current solutions and are looking at your Offerings as an alternative. Their interest is real, but they lack the true incentive to change. They really just want things to remain as they are, but something has made them nervous. They are looking for an insurance policy. They want something they can quickly "pull off the shelf" if their current solution stops being viable. These customers can be both expensive (because they show interest you can commit a lot of resources to moving things ahead with them) and demoralizing (when they qualify your solution but won't buy).

If Enthusiasts and Insurance Policy Buyers don't typically sustain an OPPORTUNITY, who does?

If you're a parent, you know that you will do _anything_ to stop your child from crying. You feel your child's pain. Parents of Screaming Babies are the customers of OPPORTUNITIES you're looking to find. What's the screaming baby your target customers are trying to pacify? (Note: Pain doesn't always come from needing a different or better solution, sometimes the screaming is simply because they want it cheaper – especially in mature markets.)

Are you really addressing a pain point? Or is it just the latest technology to be explored and understood? Or a "just in case back-up?" Probe hard to understand the pain and ensure the interest you're seeing isn't just enthusiasm for something new.

> What's really wrong with the way it's being done now? Do they need a different solution like the parent of a screaming child?
>
> How will you make your customers more successful?
>
> How much will they value and pay you for it?

Does your offer present the same level of importance to your customers as a bottle or new diaper for the parents of a screaming baby? Or is it nice to have – something they might need someday – an insurance policy. Yes, there is a market for insurance policies, but the adoption rate is much slower. The customers who are parents of a screaming baby want to buy, and buy now, and they (almost) don't care what it costs. They want the pain to stop for their baby, and for themselves. These are the customers you want to be serving. Make sure the OPPORTUNITIES you select are targeting Parents of Screaming Babies and you'll travel your desired road much faster.

It's not as hard to find Screaming Babies as you might think. As mentioned, the same benefits at a lower cost (thus higher value for the customer) is the easiest example but competing on lower cost may not be attractive to you. What else could you look for?

Parents know once you have a child it's impossible to imagine the world without them. The same is true for your Offerings. Once your customers have learned about or tried your solution can they imagine their world without it? If not you're on the right track.

Can you imagine your life without a microwave or smart phone? Few consumers would use a bank without access to ATMs or, increasingly, on-line services. And not every solution needs to be highly technical. The curved shower rod fixed the screaming problem of a shower curtain clinging to you with a couple extra inches of metal or plastic and a slight bend. Now, nearly every hotel, and many homes, have rapidly adopted this simple solution. None of these were the "latest and greatest" or something you'd want "just in case". They addressed a problem to make your life easier or experience better and now you can't imagine living without them. Choose OPPORTUNITIES that do the same for your customers.

What's your plan to win?

Next, what's your ADVANTAGE over competition? David had a plan when he volunteered to fight Goliath. He knew both what his ADVANTAGE was and his opponent's weakness. The same should be true for your strategy.

> What's your plan to win?
>
> Why can you provide or achieve it better than someone else?
>
> What's to prevent someone else from copying, replacing, or improving on what you offer?

One way to identify ADVANTAGE is to challenge assumptions. Reprieving my three examples: leaders of Amazon, Google, and Walmart each challenged an industry assumption, and redefined the category to their ADVANTAGE in the process:

> Amazon – you had to carry big inventories to be a bookstore.
>
> Google – Internet search was only for techies (and an easy way to search the Internet wasn't needed or valuable).
>
> Walmart – small towns couldn't support department stores.

One common assumption is that ADVANTAGE comes from the product or technology behind it.

However, that assumption isn't always true. ADVANTAGE often has nothing to do with the product itself. Let's look again at those three example companies.

Amazon's ADVANTAGE doesn't come from its e-commerce business model – plenty of companies have that – but from its flywheel business model. The more shoppers come to the website, the more sellers join the platform to provide those customers with products and services. The larger number of vendors increases competition among them, decreasing prices for customers on the website. And the lower prices keep customers coming back to platform. *The cycle repeats itself over and over again, each time getting more powerful.*

Google's ADVANTAGE came from a business system that allowed them to combine a simpler user search experience with algorithms that fed user data to an advertising business model. And like the Amazon flywheel, *the system got better as customers used it over and over again* enabling better algorithms and better targeting of advertising.

The heart of Walmart's ADVANTAGE wasn't the size or the location of its stores, it was the efficiencies it built into its supply chain – and *how those were integrated into its business system*.

Notice the pattern? It isn't the product or technology that's creating the ADVANTAGE. It's a well-conceived, integrated business model and design, which can be much harder for competition to replicate.

And that brings us to the **"D"** in ROAD. How do we DESIGN ADVANTAGE into the business?

Questions to answer about your ADVANTAGE

Have you discussed, debated, and defined:
- Whether your target customers are technology enthusiasts, insurance policy buyers or parents of screaming babies?
- How and why you are making them more successful?
- What value you are creating for them and how much they will pay you for it?
- Your plan to win the OPPORTUNITIES?
- Your plan to keep the OPPORTUNITIES you win from competition copying, doing it better or taking them from you?

Have you:
- Explored the consequences of your choices?
- Defined your critical assumptions?

Tools to help define your ADVANTAGE

SWOT analysis
Customer analysis
Competitor analysis
Perceptual mapping
Blue Ocean analysis
Porter Five Forces model

Chapter Four: (D)esign

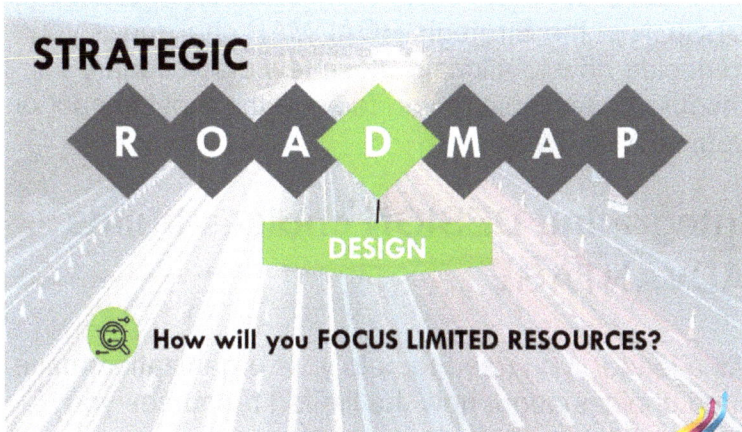

Everyone has limited resources

Let's start with a couple of givens:

1) No individual or organization is blessed with unlimited resources.

2) Every business (or organization needing to account for themselves) must commit resources to required activities that unfortunately do not help build an ADVANTAGE that enables you to win and keep OPPORTUNITIES, so you can arrive at your RESULTS on time. (Apologies to the accountants, but few organizations have accounting efforts that create ADVANTAGE).

The resources available to you to actually build ADVANTAGE are precious – so you must make the most of what's available.

DESIGN in the Strategic ROADMAP challenges you to decide how to allocate those few discretionary resources available to you to have the most impact on your ADVANTAGE.

Integrating DESIGN choices builds ADVANTAGE

As a leader, you need to help your organization make hard choices about how the limited resources you have available will be focused to create your ADVANTAGE. This involves making choices about three categories of DESIGN activities:

■ **Internal business configuration**: how you organize, your processes, and how you make money

■ **Offerings**: products and services you offer

■ **Customer Interface**: your brand and go-to-market choices

Let's look more closely at the elements of these three aspects of business DESIGN.

INTEGRATING DESIGN CHOICES BUILDS ADVANTAGE

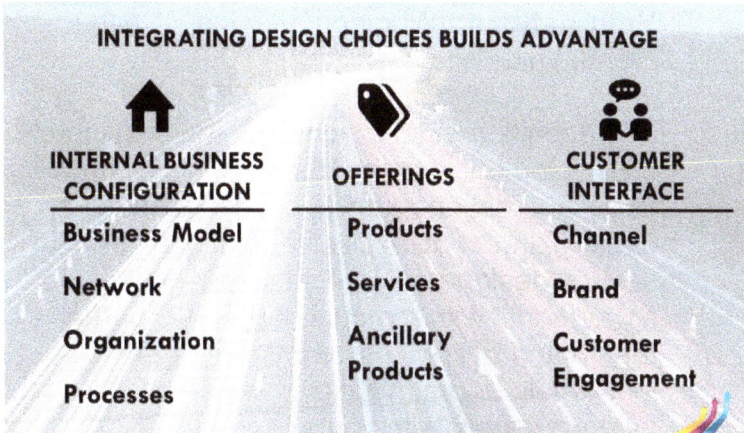

INTERNAL BUSINESS CONFIGURATION	OFFERINGS	CUSTOMER INTERFACE
Business Model	Products	Channel
Network	Services	Brand
Organization	Ancillary Products	Customer Engagement
Processes		

Internal Business Configuration

You'll need to make critical choices about your organization's business systems and processes in four critical Internal Business DESIGN elements:

1) **Your business model:** How will you make money?

   Most organizations sell products or services. Some sell at premium prices, some at "everyday low prices". Other organizations offer systems, think Microsoft Office or Google's G-Suite. Still others sell subscriptions, creating a recurring revenue stream. Your energy company and taxi services use a "metered usage" model. Your financial adviser most likely uses an hourly, fixed fee or commission approach. Christie's and Sotheby's conduct auctions and are paid commissions based on the sales price – a success fee. Each option has trade-offs. What's right for you?

2) **Your network:** Who do you connect with to create value?

   All franchisers and franchisees have intimately connected business systems. Walmart has deep connections with its suppliers and supply chain. Target has exclusive relationships with several designers. Most major airlines have agreements with regional carriers as part of their hub and spoke systems. Are there individuals or organizations whose success is interdependent with yours?

3) **Your organizational structure and culture:** How do you organize your talent, assets and decision making to create the environment you need to succeed?

   The military uses a hierarchy. Amway uses direct selling. Universities organize around colleges. Some organizations are highly centralized, others very decentralized. W.L. Gore has a "lattice" organizational structure that relies on a unique culture and individual leadership. Every structure, like every choice, has trade-offs, what are yours?

4) **Your processes:** How efficient, effective, or proprietary are your activities?

   Many companies have adopted lean manufacturing, just-in-time supply chains, 6-sigma, and other approaches to creating ADVANTAGE through more efficient and effective processes. Others use an aggressive approach to intellectual property – including patents or trade secrets (think Coca-Cola). Outsourcing and crowdsourcing have become ways of competing faster and with fewer resources. How does your company use processes to create ADVANTAGE?

Offerings

Your organization's Offering decisions make up the second category of DESIGN and generally fall into the following three areas:

1) **Your products:** How do you distinguish yourself for your customers and from competition?

    Performance, functionality, design, and cost are common choices that need to be made about your product Offerings. More recently, Environmental, Social and Governance (ESG) factors regarding products, how they are produced and how organizations (including their supply chain) behave have become a critical part of value. Is there something special or unique about your products?

2) **Your services:** How do you support your customers in selecting and using your products to enhance their value?

    Warranties and guarantees, maintenance and supplemental service plans, product information and training, and try before you buy are examples of services that enhance the benefit and value of your products for customers. Do you offer services that enhance the benefit or experience your customers receive and value?

3) **Ancillary Products or Product Systems:** Have you considered complimentary products or offerings that create enhanced systems?

Product bundles are an example of product systems: razors are often sold with refill blades, shampoos often with conditioners. Modular systems are available for stereo systems, bedrooms, and office furniture, just to name a few categories, where components can be used individually or as a completed system. Many websites and software programs also provide plug-ins or extensions that enable them to work seamlessly with other systems. All of these are designed to complement and enhance the value customers derive from the core offering. What compliments your products and services? Should these be part of your Offerings?

Customer Interface

The remaining set of DESIGN choices involve how you interface with your customers, also falling into three key areas:

1) **Your channel:** How do you deliver your Offerings to customers and users?

Direct sales and distribution are two of the most well-known types of channels.

Distribution options could include agents and resellers. E-commerce and on-demand are among the more recent channel possibilities, sometimes paired with brick-and-mortar stores. Uber Eats, DoorDash and Grubhub will all deliver food to your door, at almost any time of day. Webinars, on-line communities, and social media have become major channels for both influencers (a business of its own) and brands. How do customers obtain your Offerings? What impact does this have on their experiences and value?

2) **Your Brand:** How do you represent yourself, your business, and your Offerings?

Your brand is your expression of who you are, what you do, why it matters and why someone should do business with you. It expresses your values and the desirable characteristics of your business to build credibility and a relationship with your customers. You don't only choose what it is to build ADVANTAGE, but how to use it yourself and how to use or lend it to others with brand extensions, co-branding, private labeling or other options to extend what you want to establish. Is your brand appropriately reflected in the choices you're making? How can you make it clearer and more valuable for your customers?

3) **Your customer engagement:** How do you chose to engage with your customers, before, during and after the sale?

Disney, Four Seasons Hotels and Nordstrom are examples of engagement on a highly personalized level. Budget airlines are examples on the discount level – you trade off a commodity or highly non-personalized experience for a significantly lower price. Loyalty programs provide improved experiences for heavy users. Harley Davidson is well known for sponsoring events which build community among their brand followers. Restaurants may offer cooking experiences with their chefs or tables in their kitchens to enhance their customer experiences and relationships. Are the ways your customer engages with your business intentional, consistent, and helping you succeed?

These ten business DESIGN choices can be sources of ADVANTAGE, especially if you combine them in ways that make them difficult for competitors to duplicate. Recall that in Chapter 3, we discussed how ADVANTAGE often comes from more than product or technology and how the business model and design created a distinct, clear, and difficult to replicate ADVANTAGE for Amazon, Google, and Walmart. You can do the same, but it will require consideration and choices. Southwest Airlines does this exceedingly well in the discount airline market – Chapter 8 shows how they do it. For additional examples and detail in how you might approach DESIGN, Keeley[13] uses a similar approach he defines as "innovation" and gives

---

[13] Keeley, Larry, et Al. *Ten Types of Innovation: The Discipline of Building Breakthroughs*. Hoboken, Nj, John Wiley & Sons Inc, 2013, p128-187.

several examples in part five of his book that may provide you with ideas.

Leveraging Resources

It may be apparent from either the Network element in DESIGN, or the PARTNER in ROADMAP, that you can choose to engage resources outside of your organization, allowing you to concentrate your resources on the elements you can build and integrate to improve your ADVANTAGE. Major airlines do this with regional carriers, handing off the shorter, less traveled "spoke" flights to smaller cities to their regional partners and concentrating on larger aircraft and longer routes.

Determine which few elements can most significantly be combined to contribute to your ADVANTAGE and resource them accordingly. It will be tough. There will be hard choices to make to focus and integrate them to deliver the most ADVANTAGE for your resource commitment, but this work will pay off on the journey.

Questions to answer about your DESIGN

- Have you made clear decisions about all 10 elements of DESIGN?
- Are you clear which elements are most important to creating your ADVANTAGE for customers?
- Do your resource allocations and plans focus on these most important elements?

- Do your choices work together to deliver ADVANTAGE intentionally and consistently to your customer?
- Will this combination of elements be difficult for competitors to copy or defeat?
- Have you considered possibilities for Networks or Partners that might create additional leverage?

Have you:
- Explored the consequences of your choices?
- Defined your critical assumptions?

Tools to help define your DESIGN

Keeley's Ten Types of Innovation
Resource-based view model
Value chain analysis
McKinsey 7S framework

Part 2: Shifting to Execution: The MAP

Focused on Execution: The MAP

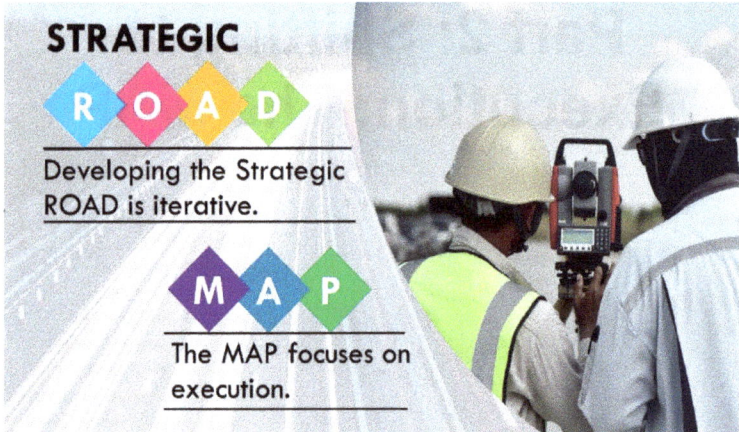

You've defined your ROAD to success.

The RESULTS are clear. You've selected the OPPORTUNITIES for getting there. You've determined how to create ADVANTAGE. And your business DESIGN ensures your activities and resource investments are integrated so you get the most impact from them.

Now it's time to move on from creating the "ROAD" and embark on the journey.

The "MAP" focuses on execution – getting to success. So, let's get going.

Chapter Five: (M)ilestones

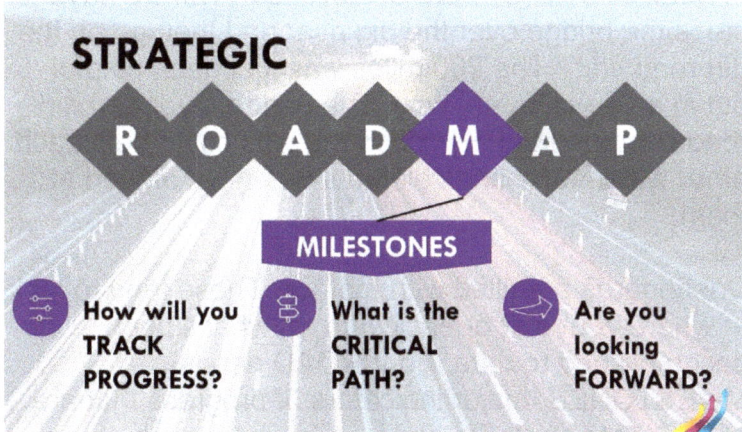

STRATEGIC ROADMAP

MILESTONES

How will you **TRACK PROGRESS?**   What is the **CRITICAL PATH?**   Are you looking **FORWARD?**

Managing Progress

Every journey has markers that allow you to confirm you're headed in the right direction and assess how fast you're moving. Today's digital world provides the opportunity for endless streams of data and information, and many organizations have dashboards to monitor every possible operational metric. Including data in your daily decisions is an absolute necessity, but often the metrics associated with dashboards aren't helpful to assess progress toward your desired RESULTS.

"Are we there yet?" As the parent of four young children, family trips were both enjoyable and exhausting. We'd plan the journey and load the car with great enthusiasm. Once underway, it usually took about 15 minutes before someone would ask the inevitable question. A quick answer of "of course not, we have 200 miles to go" would result in another "are we there yet" about five minutes later. This cycle would repeat until at least one and preferably a series of MILESTONE(S) were established. "No, we have to cross the bridge over the big river and then go on the dirt road first." The 200 miles was just data, helpful but in a very different way. The bridge, river and dirt road became MILESTONES the kids could help each other watch for – and celebrate when we arrived at them.

Dashboards are filled with metrics. These tend to look at where you're at or backward, at what's been accomplished to date. Your ROAD needs MILESTONES, major indicators of progress that are ahead that your team can look for, help each other work toward, and celebrate when they've been achieved. MILESTONES are in categories like the metrics you use to manage the business every day:

■ Financial

■ Customer and market

■ Technical or R&D innovations

■ Product enhancements and new introductions

But remember, you want MILESTONES to represent significant points on the journey *ahead* (we need to....). Metrics look back at what *happened* yesterday or even today (we did....).

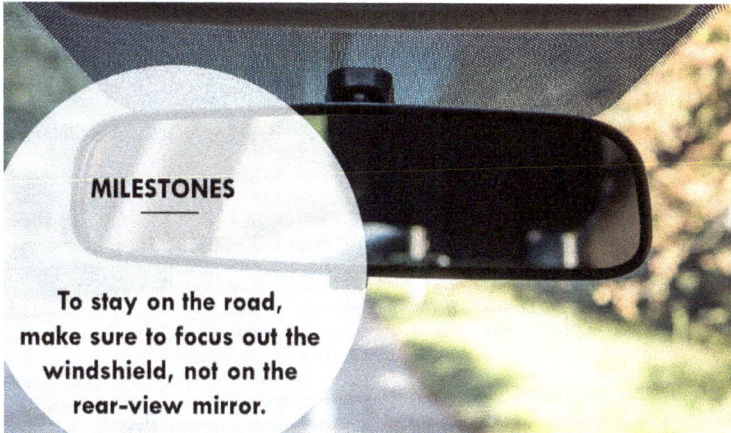

MILESTONES

To stay on the road,
make sure to focus out the
windshield, not on the
rear-view mirror.

Metrics, like miles travelled, are looking in the "rear-view mirror". If you drive by looking in the rear-view mirror, it won't be long before you end up somewhere you didn't intend. Hits on your webpage or likes on LinkedIn or Facebook are vanity metrics. They might help you feel good, but for most businesses they don't indicate true progress on the critical path to success. When not correctly used Employee Satisfaction surveys or Net Promoter Scores can also be vanity metrics. They look backward, and scores are often results of factors not directly affected by management efforts.

Hitting a significant revenue number can demonstrate real progress in many cases but recognize that revenue is a "rear-view mirror" metric a lot like miles travelled. Lots of things must happen before revenue starts rolling in or grows. Identify those things and make the important ones MILESTONES.

MILESTONES are best when they are "Windshield metrics"; ones that you can see coming and help you know you're on the right road and making good time to where you want to be, like the bridge, river, and dirt road. Your MILESTONES should have you looking through the windshield at where you're going, not looking in the rear-view mirror at where you've been.

MILESTONES will be different for every business. Often, they are significant things that need to be learned, earned, committed, decided, achieved, overcome, or built.

At the end of each chapter in Part 1, you were asked about the critical assumptions you were making. Now reframe these into hypotheses you can test or questions you can answer. Many of these will be critical MILESTONES you need to address to be sure you are on the right ROAD to success.

These frequently involve something or someone's action that is not in your control. You can't make your customers commit to a trial or sign a contract. You generally don't control technical or R&D innovations. A third-party endorsement or specification involves someone else acting in your behalf. What are the events on your critical path that involve something outside of your control? Arriving at these are often significant MILESTONES. Taking the time to determine what these are in advance will not only help you ensure you're progressing; it will help make sure the team is aware of and working on achieving them.

Iterating between working backward from your desired RESULTS and forward from where you are today can also help identify MILESTONES.

And remember the point earlier about not going alone and being inspirational? The ROAD to success can be long and hard. Make sure you use MILESTONES to celebrate and keep the team inspired when you achieve them.

At this point you may be looking for more concrete examples of MILESTONES and metrics. I'll confess, that's really hard to provide generically. Because often they can be the same. But if you've paid close attention, you'll note that the difference would be where they are relative to where you are in your journey. MILESTONES are still in front of you (something you still need to achieve) and metrics are behind you (something you've already achieved). Spend the majority of your management time and attention on where you want to be and how to get there, not where you've already been. A glance in the rear-view mirror can be helpful for learning and improving, but to get where you want to go most of your attention needs to be through the windshield on the MILESTONES for the ROAD ahead.

Questions to answer about your MILESTONES

Have you:
- Identified significant things that need to be learned, earned, committed, decided, achieved, overcome, built, or determined and when it needs to be done to achieve the RESULTS on time?
- Identified significant phases of the journey and when they end/begin?

Have you:
- Removed vanity metrics and focused through the windshield?
- Used your critical assumptions to develop hypotheses you can test and confirm or questions you need to answer?

Tools to help manage your MILESTONES

Wide variety of task and project management software and apps
Gantt charts
Balanced scorecards

Chapter Six: (A)ction Plans

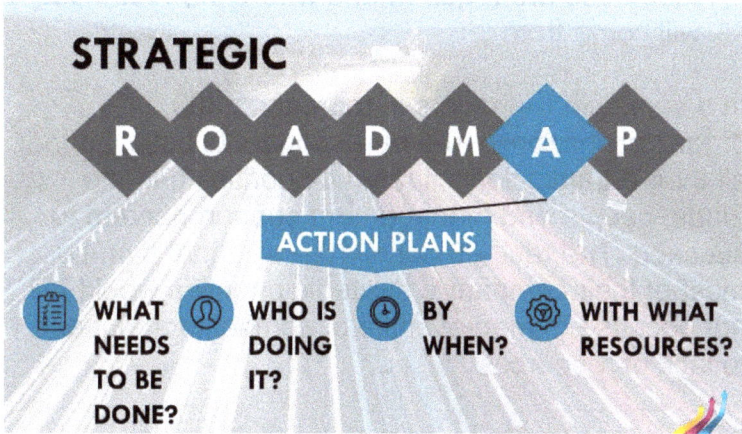

Getting it done

Who is responsible for doing what – by when? Having identified your critical MILESTONES, most organizations will be able to lay out ACTION PLANS and accountability to achieve them. But that isn't enough to ensure success. It's about more than having the right people that understand the plans. One critical factor is still missing – *with what resources*?

When developing ACTION PLANS be sure to:

➢ Keep them focused on achieving the strategic MILESTONES.

➢ Involve those who will need to execute them to secure buy-in and accountability. This helps with being inspiring by addressing the "why."

➢ Structure them in achievable chunks with specific roles and responsibilities and clarity on what resources are required and where the resources will come from.

In a survey of managers in more than 300 organizations, only 10% of respondents believed that all their organization's strategic priorities had the funds, people and management support needed to succeed. The rest – 9 out of 10 – said that some or most of their company's strategic priorities would fail, not because of market shifts or competitors, but due to lack of resources.[14]

If you don't want to be part of the 90%, or risk your strategic priorities failing, ACTION PLANS need to explicitly consider resource availability.

After you've made the resources available, hold regular reviews and updates. Keep those reviews looking through the windshield at progress toward the MILESTONES – especially if you build in assumptions or stretch – not in the rear-view mirror at what was or wasn't done.

---

[14]-Results from an online survey designed to assess an organization's capacity to execute its strategy administered to 302 organizations between 2012 and 2017. "The Strategic Agility Project: How to Develop Strategy for Execution" Donald Sull, Stefano Turconi, Charles Sull and James Yoder *MIT Sloan Management Review*

Remember the pit crew? They need enough tires and gas to finish the race. If the crew is short tires or gas, everyone needs to adjust and the sooner it's recognized and communicated the better.

Circumstances change quickly and can dictate that the driver conserves fuel or the car runs with just two fresh tires instead of four new ones for a few laps to get to the checkered flag. During your regular reviews keep an eye on conditions and assumptions for changes which may require refreshing the strategy or re-allocating resources. Or maybe the changes will allow you to skip a pit stop and accelerate the plan.

A best practice during reviews is to conduct a Continue / Start / Stop / Change discussion as you review the ACTION PLANS. Given the progress, conditions and any changes that need to be considered, what ACTIONS should be continued, started, stopped, or changed? This helps keep you focused through the windshield on the ROAD ahead and what will help you get to the MILESTONES and RESULTS rather than just checking off items on an action register. Then re-assess the resources for each ACTION and make sure the team has enough tires and gas or make the necessary adjustments, so you get to your destination on time.

And don't forget to consider how PARTNERS might help you along the way.

Questions to answer about your ACTION PLANS

- Are they focused on your strategic MILESTONES?
- Are the ACTIONS specific, measurable, achievable, relevant, and time-bound (SMART)?
- Are critical assumptions clearly identified, and ACTIONS to test, validate or update them included?
- Are the accountabilities clear and agreed upon?
- Have the resources required been agreed to – and committed from the source that has them?
- Have you considered how PARTNERS can help?
- Do you have a plan for communicating issues or changes as they occur and appropriately adjusting the ACTION PLANS?
- Do you have a plan for reviewing the ACTION PLANS, including the availability of resources regularly?

Have you:
- Explored the consequences of your choices?
- Involved those who will need to execute them to secure buy-in and accountability?
- Structured them in achievable chunks with specific roles and responsibilities?

Tools to help manage your ACTION PLANS

The web is loaded with action register templates
that you may consider or modify. This
reference has several.[2]
Gantt charts
RACI diagrams
Project management software

---

[2]TemplateLab. "49 Great Action Item Templates (MS Word &
Excel) ▷ TemplateLab." TemplateLab.Com, 31 July 2019,
templatelab.com/action-item-templates/. Accessed 7 May 2020.

Chapter Seven: (P)artners

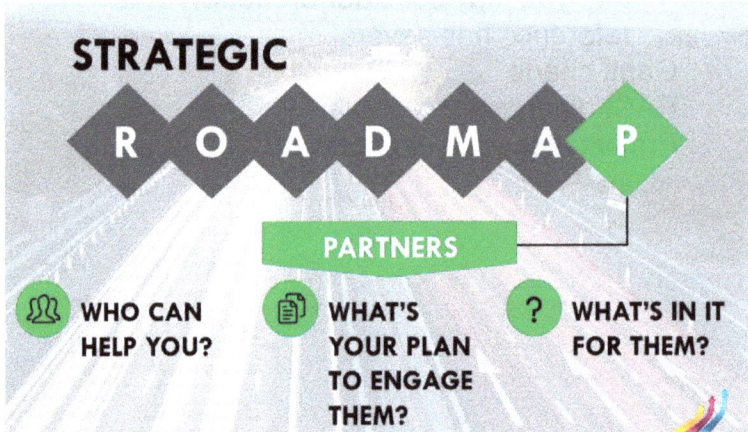

Who can help?

On a big trip you need hotels, gas stations, restaurants, and other vendors – help from or with resources you can't carry with you. Most of us have preferred or frequent user relationships with many suppliers that make our trips easier, cheaper, and more enjoyable. It's easy to identify who's helpful on a road trip.

The same is true in your business. PARTNERS can help you get to your RESULTS easier, faster or with less investment on your part. Organizations already engaged with you may have more interest in seeing you succeed than you may have realized. Maybe it's those who provide you:

- Education – training
- Banking – financing and financial services
- Associations – networking, education, standards, certifications, regulations
- Logistics
- Suppliers, Distributors/Reps
- Existing or Past customers

Consider who is involved in developing or supporting your:

- Business Configurations
- Offerings: Products, Services, Ancillary products
- Customer experiences

Identify who among these or other organizations can help you succeed – determine how they could also benefit and develop a plan to engage them.

Keys to a successful collaboration

Establishing a successful PARTNERShip starts by doing the homework. Once you've identified who can help you, develop a specific plan for working with them.

Clearly define your objectives for the relationship before you engage them. Remember, you want to be intentional. A common mistake when establishing collaborations is to not be clear and intentional about what you want from the engagement. Once you sit down with the other party, conversations have a way of taking on a life of their own and you can end up somewhere accidentally. Know what you want from the relationship, what you're willing to bring to it and where you draw the line before you engage the other side.

You can start this homework by researching the company and considering their point-of-view on the potential collaboration.

Determine the desired duration of the engagement and the level of formality it should take – is a handshake or a contract more appropriate? If the collaboration involves high levels of commitment, investment, risk, or (intellectual or other) assets, understand how you would agree to exit the agreement before you even start to establish it. The "divorce" or "pre-nuptial" conditions might be the most important ones you prepare. Then for most collaborations, draft a 3-column table. Label the first column "terms" and the other columns with the name of each party. Complete the table with what you expect each party will give and get for every "term" that is significant in the relationship. Highlight the terms that are your "must haves" and "won't agree to" or "dealbreakers." This preparation, before engaging the other party, will lead to better discussions or negotiations and ultimately more successful collaborations.

Another key to a winning PARTNERShip is ensuring that both parties are aligned around shared objectives and expectations. Collaborations are a two-way street, so first make sure you both want to be on the same street. Then make sure you agree on what each party is expecting to give and take from the relationship. While most everyone agrees that there needs to be give and take, PARTNERShips fail when one party believes the other is doing more taking.

Goals, roles, and contributions for each side should be thoroughly discussed, clarified, and agreed upon. Before you're done, make sure you discuss and agree on the "divorce" or "pre-nuptial" conditions. Although it's often difficult to address since everyone is counting on success, this may be one of the most important elements of your agreement.

If all the conditions align for a collaboration, make sure you also identify who the champion(s) for the relationship are on the other side. This should be the key individual(s) who understands, supports, and even advocates for your interests and those of the collaboration inside your PARTNERS organization. A change of the champion who had the ability to support and commit to you can mean the end of an otherwise wonderful relationship if there isn't someone else who can step in that understands and aligns with you. This can happen at any point in the collaboration, even well after the relationship is established. Stay aware of personal and business interests that may change over time with your PARTNERS.

PARTNERS can be a valuable tool to getting to your RESULTS. Invest in them as intentionally as you do other parts of your strategy. They can make your journey easier, faster, cheaper, and more enjoyable.

Questions to answer about your PARTNERS

Have you discussed, debated, and defined:
- How a PARTNER can help you get to your RESULTS easier, faster or with less investment on your part?

- Your targeted PARTNER(s)?
- Exactly what you need from them and what's in it for them?
- What you're willing to bring to the relationship and where you draw the line?
- The pre-nuptial or divorce terms you can accept?

Have you:
- Ensured your potential PARTNER wants to go down the same street as you?
- Clarified and agreed upon goals, roles, contributions, and divorce conditions for both sides?
- Ensured you have the right champion(s) in your PARTNER's organization, and who might be her/his successors?
- Defined your critical assumptions?

Tools to help define your PARTNERS

Pyramid of Alliances
Partnership Preservation Checklist[3]
10 questions to make your strategic
partnership successful[4]

---

[3] Charles D. Kerns, PhD. "Preserve and Strengthen a Business Partnership." *Graziadio Business Review*, vol. 1999 Volume 2 Issue 4, no. 4, 13 Aug. 2010, gbr.pepperdine.edu/2010/08/preserve-and-strengthen-a-business-partnership/.

[4] Lancefield, David, and Jagan Rao. "Telecoms, Media and Technology Strategic Partnerships: The Real Deal?" 2010.

That's the Strategic ROADMAP

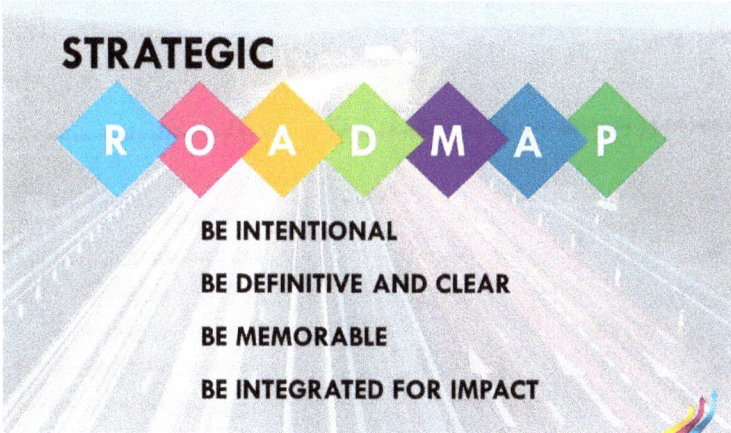

That's the Strategic ROADMAP. It's an integrated, intentional, definitive, and clear path to success that you and your team can remember and leverage every day.

So, let's look at a case study.

Chapter Eight:
Southwest Airlines
An Example Case

Southwest's Desired Results

SOUTHWEST AIRLINES VISION:
TO BECOME THE WORLD'S MOST LOVED, MOST FLOWN, AND MOST PROFITABLE AIRLINE

In 1971, Southwest Airlines operated four planes out of little Love Field in Dallas, Texas, to two destinations: Houston and San Antonio. And they had the seemingly audacious desire to become the world's most loved, flown and most profitable airline. The vision was bold and quantifiable. It lacked a specific time frame, but it was clear that this was something founder Herb Kelleher intended on achieving. And Kelleher's bold and audacious vision was inspiring for many who wanted to join him.

Southwest's Opportunities

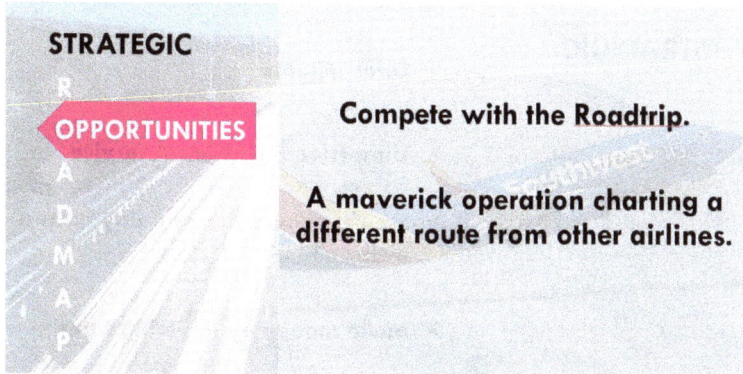

STRATEGIC

OPPORTUNITIES

Compete with the Roadtrip.

A maverick operation charting a different route from other airlines.

To achieve this vision Southwest chose to compete not with other airlines, but with driving, initially between Dallas, Houston, and San Antonio. This was consistent with the capabilities they had (just four planes), and it also provided the OPPORTUNITY for significant growth.

Clearly, if Southwest could compete effectively with the road trip in a manner that was significantly different than other airlines there was sufficient potential to achieve their vision. This OPPORTUNITY could allow them to achieve their desired RESULT.

So how did they go about creating ADVANTAGE to capture the OPPORTUNITY?

Southwest's Advantage

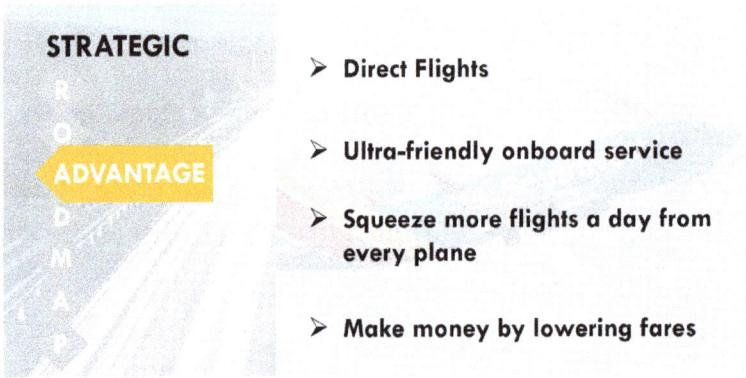

STRATEGIC

ADVANTAGE

> Direct Flights

> Ultra-friendly onboard service

> Squeeze more flights a day from every plane

> Make money by lowering fares

An airline wishing to compete effectively against driving would have to do things very differently. To achieve their OPPORTUNITY Southwest focused on providing fun, direct travel at low costs.

Ultra-friendly onboard service (clearly different from other airlines and consistent with the fun of a road trip) made the airline different and was a key part of making Southwest attractive for customers. To be even more compelling, Southwest focused on reducing ticket prices, in part by cutting out the middleman, the travel agents, and requiring customers to purchase tickets directly from Southwest. While this was new at the time, the savings passed along to customers provided motivation for the change in customer buying behavior.

Operating differently than other airlines was a critical factor of the strategy for the long term. Initially, by operating only in Texas, Southwest had a cost

ADVANTAGE by avoiding regulations faced by competitive airlines who operated beyond the state.

Direct travel (like a road trip) and being super-efficient with their most expensive assets, the planes, delivered more revenue per plane, reduced costs and made the strategy extremely difficult for Southwest's competitors to respond to with their "hub and spoke" models. It also produced lower costs for Southwest and their customers helping to create a sustainable ADVANTAGE and way to keep the OPPORTUNITY once Southwest won it.

The combination of these approaches would allow Southwest to make money while lowering fares and positioned them to compete consistently with a road trip, fueling growth.

To consistently create these ADVANTAGES, Southwest had to think differently about how to DESIGN their airline.

Southwest's Design

Integrated DESIGN choices
built ADVANTAGE

The ADVANTAGE Southwest sought to create led to
DESIGN choices that were radical for the airline
industry.

Low costs

In business configuration, Southwest's choices to
achieve low costs included the decision to operate
only Boeing 737s. This minimized direct costs such as
the inventory of replacement parts and indirect costs
that includes training for maintenance and operations
staff. It also meant any pilot could fly any plane,
simplifying operations and staffing.
The company was also an early adopter of fuel
hedging and equipping planes with winglets to save
fuel costs.

The airline's focus on fast turnarounds enabled higher
utilization of their most expensive asset, the planes.
This effected Southwest's business configuration,
product and service offering, and customer interface
decisions.

High utilization made roles and job requirements especially important. Incentivizing all employees to assist in quickly and efficiently turning aircraft was key to achieving higher utilization. Pilots, gate agents and flight attendants would all need to pitch in to clean and turn the plane, rather than waiting for an airport cleaning staff to arrive and do the job. This required the company to avoid the highly restrictive organizational structure and contract constraints other airlines operated under, effecting business configuration choices of organizational structure and processes.

Flying only to secondary airports (like Love Field instead of DFW in Dallas or Midway instead of O'Hare in Chicago) resulted in less congestion and thus faster turnarounds, clearly effecting the company's offerings for customers, but consistent with their intent on achieving higher utilization and integrated with achieving lower costs.

The quest for fast turnarounds also had an impact on the customer interface: the open seating and boarding practices were both significant departures from the approach used by other airlines and gave Southwest an ADVANTAGE loading and turning their aircraft.

The Fun of a Road trip

Southwest flight attendants became known for transforming mundane pre-flight instructions into YouTube worthy shareable events. Their ability to inject humor into the announcement was an intentional part of delivering the strategy by emulating the fun of a road trip. A fun and better customer experience was intentional, influencing the decisions on organizational design. As already mentioned, the company utilized a highly flexible workforce. They further extended this flexibility into human resources choices which made "fit with the culture" a critical criterion of the hiring practices.

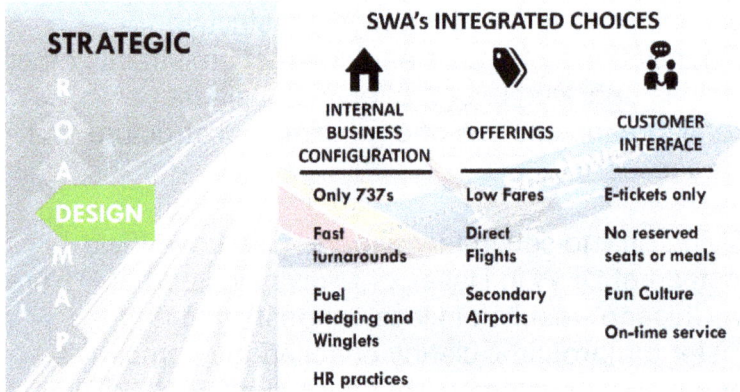

STRATEGIC	SWA's INTEGRATED CHOICES		
	INTERNAL BUSINESS CONFIGURATION	OFFERINGS	CUSTOMER INTERFACE
DESIGN	Only 737s	Low Fares	E-tickets only
	Fast turnarounds	Direct Flights	No reserved seats or meals
	Fuel Hedging and Winglets	Secondary Airports	Fun Culture
	HR practices		On-time service

Note how the elements summarized above integrate to provide lower costs, higher utilization, more fun and efficient travel for passengers and how they make it difficult for other airlines to copy. At the time, many of these concepts, such as only allowing passengers to purchase e-tickets and not using travel agents were bold and innovative! Even the use of fuel saving winglets across the fleet was an airline first.

Southwest made intentional choices to DESIGN their business to operate differently and create the ADVANTAGE needed capture the OPPORTUNITY they wanted to achieve their desired RESULTS in a highly competitive industry.

Southwest's Milestones and Actions

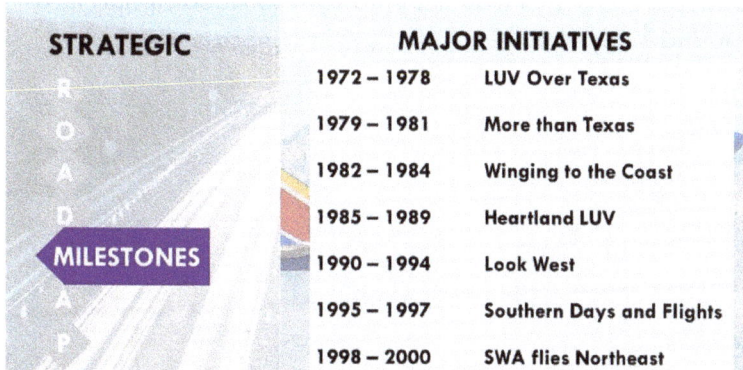

STRATEGIC	MAJOR INITIATIVES	
R	1972 – 1978	LUV Over Texas
O	1979 – 1981	More than Texas
A	1982 – 1984	Winging to the Coast
D	1985 – 1989	Heartland LUV
MILESTONES	1990 – 1994	Look West
A	1995 – 1997	Southern Days and Flights
P	1998 – 2000	SWA flies Northeast

For clarity, the Strategic ROADMAP framework was developed well after Southwest began on their journey, so we are applying the framework in retrospect here as we consider the strategic ROAD Southwest defined and the MAP that described the execution of the strategy along the journey.

The "major initiatives" listed in their company history on their website make it clear that Southwest focused on MILESTONES on the road to their desired RESULT and give an indication of the phases of growth they journeyed through. In 1975, Southwest began operating flights to various additional cities within Texas, and in 1979 it began flying to neighboring states. Service to the east and the southeast started in the 1990s. It is clear that the company identified the pathway to growth and focused specific ACTION PLANS to achieving the related MILESTONES.

Southwest could not have expanded beyond Texas in the late 70s if they didn't have the financial strength or the planes to accommodate that growth. They matched the resources required to the MILESTONES and ACTION PLANS they sought to accomplish in a focused approach.

Southwest's Partners

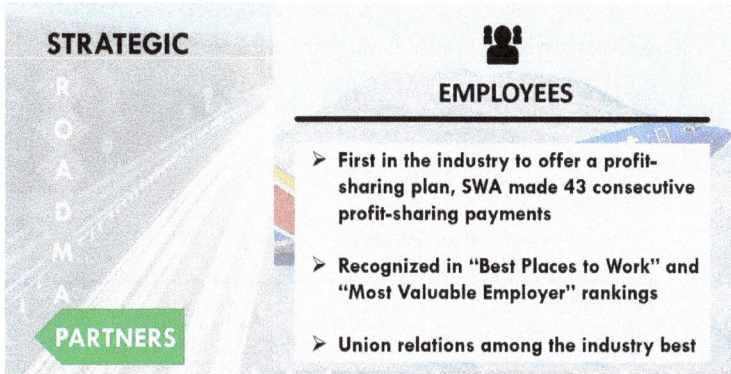

STRATEGIC
R
O
A
D
M
A
PARTNERS

EMPLOYEES

➤ First in the industry to offer a profit-sharing plan, SWA made 43 consecutive profit-sharing payments

➤ Recognized in "Best Places to Work" and "Most Valuable Employer" rankings

➤ Union relations among the industry best

Clearly Southwest employees were critical to achieving the OPPORTUNITIES and ADVANTAGES.

Employees were essential to creating the culture of "fun" – recall the humorous on-board safety instructions – and deliver an exceptional customer experience. In addition, the willingness of flight attendants, gate agents and even pilots to help clean the planes, board passengers, and turn the plane quickly and on-time was necessary to optimize asset utilization and ensure low costs.

What was in it for them? As part of the business DESIGN, Southwest created the first profit sharing plan in the airline industry, PARTNERing with their employees. This plan paid employees significantly for over 40 years, and Southwest has a history of having some of the best employee relations in an industry that is known for terrible union relationships. Southwest engaged employees differently creating an energetic culture that supported and may even have been a strong reason for the company's growth.

Southwest: Arrived at the Destination

The Destination: SWA Results

➢ Ranks highest in J.D. Power's 2018 NA Airline Satisfaction Study among low-cost carriers

➢ Carries approximately 20% of U.S. passengers

➢ 44 straight years of profitability, in an industry in which every other major company has gone through bankruptcy

Southwest has achieved their desired RESULT and become a major player in the US airline industry where almost every other airline has declared or come close to bankruptcy in the same period.

Of course, they didn't have the Strategic ROADMAP to use to get there, but by focusing and integrating their activities in the manner defined by the ROADMAP they've achieved impressive, industry leading success.

You've Arrived

STRATEGIC ROADMAP

An intentional, memorable approach to achieving success

You've made it to the end of this journey to explore the Strategic ROADMAP.

The integrated, intentional, definitive, and clear framework intended to provoke and inspire your planning and communicating with your team to

Be intentional
Be definitive and clear
Be memorable and
Be integrated

I hope it helps you to achieve the RESULTS and success you desire.

Andy

About the Author

Andrew L. Shafer
Strategist, Business and Brand Builder

https://www.linkedin.com/in/andyshafer/
andy@andyshafer.biz

Andy has a unique understanding of the dynamics required for success in a diverse set of public and privately held business environments, including start-ups and Fortune 50 multi-national companies. His career includes being a founder and executive at 2 leading bio-material companies, Elevance Renewable Sciences, Inc. and NatureWorks, LLC, and holding senior business leadership roles at Cargill, Inc., and The Dow Chemical Company.

Andy's background includes forming and operating joint ventures, private equity funded entities and novel business models. He brings strengths and executive level experience developing and implementing strategy, commercializing new businesses/product developments and innovations, establishing partnerships, and building brands and marketing capability in organizations. Andy is now helping large and emerging companies build their businesses and innovate, advising senior business executives at Fortune 100 companies and serving as an advisor and board member at several start-up and early stage companies.

Andy has a bachelor's degree in chemical engineering from the University of Notre Dame with an MBA from the University of Minnesota's Carlson School of Management, and a certificate in Managerial Issues in the Global Enterprise from Thunderbird School of Global Management.

www.ingramcontent.com/pod-product-compliance
Lightning Source LLC
Chambersburg PA
CBHW071110210326
41519CB00020B/6252